Collins

AQA GCSE 9-1 Maths

Maths

Higher

Higher

AQA GCSE 9-1

Workbook

Linda Couchman
and Rebecca Evans

Rethink Revision

Have you ever taken part in a quiz and thought *'I know this!'* but, despite frantically racking your brain, you just couldn't come up with the answer?

It's very frustrating when this happens but, in a fun situation, it doesn't really matter. However, in your GCSE exams, it will be essential that you can recall the relevant information quickly when you need to.

Most students think that revision is about making sure you **know** stuff. Of course, this is important, but it is also about becoming confident that you can **retain** that *stuff* over time and **recall** it quickly when needed.

Revision That Really Works

Experts have discovered that there are two techniques that help with all of these things and consistently produce better results in exams compared to other revision techniques.

Applying these techniques to your GCSE revision will ensure you get better results in your exams and will have all the relevant knowledge at your fingertips when you start studying for further qualifications, like AS and A Levels, or begin work.

It really isn't rocket science either – you simply need to:

- **test yourself** on each topic as many times as possible
- **leave a gap** between the test sessions.

Three Essential Revision Tips

1. **Use Your Time Wisely**

   - Allow yourself plenty of time.
   - Try to start revising at least six months before your exams – it's more effective and less stressful.
   - Your revision time is precious so use it wisely – using the techniques described on this page will ensure you revise effectively and efficiently and get the best results.
   - Don't waste time re-reading the same information over and over again – it's time-consuming and not effective!

2. **Make a Plan**

   - Identify all the topics you need to revise.
   - Plan at least five sessions for each topic.
   - One hour should be ample time to test yourself on the key ideas for a topic.
   - Spread out the practice sessions for each topic – the optimum time to leave between each session is about one month but, if this isn't possible, just make the gaps as big as realistically possible.

3. **Test Yourself**

   - Methods for testing yourself include: quizzes, practice questions, flashcards, past papers, explaining a topic to someone else, etc.
   - Don't worry if you get an answer wrong – provided you check what the correct answer is, you are more likely to get the same or similar questions right in future!

Visit our website for more information about the benefits of these techniques and for further guidance on how to plan ahead and make them work for you.

www.collins.co.uk/collinsGCSErevision

Contents

N Number   A Algebra   G Geometry and Measures

S Statistics   P Probability   R Ratio, Proportion and Rates of Change

Order and Value

1 **a)** Write two hundred million in standard form. 🖩

Answer _____ [1]

b) Write 6.78×10^{-4} as an ordinary number. 🖩

Answer _____ [1]

2 Work out $(1.5 \times 10^4) + (3.5 \times 10^3)$. Give your answer in standard form. 🖩

Answer _____ [3]

3 Work out the value of $\frac{(3\sqrt{m})}{y}$ where $m = 8.1 \times 10^3$ and $y = 2.7 \times 10^{-2}$

Give your answer in standard form. 🖩

Answer _____ [3]

4 If $45 \times 82 = 3690$, work out the value of: 🖩

a) 4.5×8.2

Answer _____ [1]

b) 0.045×0.82

Answer _____ [1]

5 Work out $0.8645 \div 0.5$ 🖩

Answer _____ [2]

6 If $53.\blacktriangle 4 \times 0.2 = 10.668$, work out the value of $\blacktriangle$ 🖩

Answer _____ [1]

Total Marks _____ / 13

Types of Number

1 3, 7, 9, 12, 16, 20, 31
From this list choose: 🖩

  a) Three prime numbers.   Answer _____ [1]

  b) Two numbers that are factors of 21.   Answer _____ [1]

  c) Three numbers that are multiples of 4.   Answer _____ [1]

  d) Two square numbers.   Answer _____ [1]

  e) The square root of 400.   Answer _____ [1]

2 Write 76 as a product of prime factors. 🖩

                                                  Answer _____ [2]

3 Find the highest common factor (HCF) of 684 and 468. 🖩

                                                  Answer _____ [3]

4 Subtract the sum of all the odd numbers from 1 to 999 from the sum of all the even numbers from 2 to 1000. 🖩

                                                  Answer _____ [2]

5 3797 is a special prime number because 379, 37 and 3 are all prime.

Is 2797 a special prime number? Explain your answer. 🖩

Answer _____ [2]

Total Marks _____ / 14

Basic Algebra

1 Solve the equation $\frac{2x + 4}{4} = 2$ 🖩

Answer _____ [3]

2 Work out the value of the following expression when $x = -2$ and $y = 7$: 🖩

$4xy - x^2$

Circle your answer.

52　　　　　　　　　60　　　　　　　　　−60　　　　　　　　　−52 [1]

3 Expand and simplify $3x(x - y) + y(x + 5)$

Answer _____ [2]

4 Solve $4x + 7 = 6x - 5$

Answer _____ [2]

5 Solve $\frac{2}{x} - 6 = 12$

Answer _____ [2]

6 Write $9xy - 3y^2 + 6x^2y$ in the form $ay(bx + cy + dx^2)$, where a, b, c, and d are integers.

Answer _____ [2]

Total Marks _____ / 12

Factorisation and Formulae

1 Expand $(x + 4)(x - 2)$

Answer _____ [2]

2 Factorise $2x^2 + 5x + 2$

Answer _____ [2]

3 The formula below links velocity, time and acceleration:

$v = u + at$

a) Use the formula to find the value of v when $u = 15$, $a = 2.5$ and $t = 10$.

Answer _____ [1]

b) Rearrange to make t the subject of the formula.

Answer _____ [2]

c) Find the value of t when $v = 25$, $a = 1.6$ and $u = 11$.

Answer _____ [1]

4 Rearrange the formula to make r the subject:

$p = \dfrac{3r - 1}{r + 2}$

Answer _____ [3]

Total Marks _____ / 11

Ratio and Proportion

1 If $\frac{2}{7}$ of the pupils in a class are girls, what is the ratio of boys to girls?

Answer _____ [1]

2 A coach uses 11 litres of fuel to travel 161.7km. How far can it travel on 13 litres of fuel?

Answer _____ [2]

3 £700 is divided between Sarah, John and James. Sarah has twice as much as John and John has three times as much as James.

How much does Sarah receive?

Answer _____ [2]

4 Simplify 15 millilitres : 3 litres

Answer _____ [1]

5 When an apple falls from a tree, the distance (d) that it falls is proportional to the square of the time (t) taken to reach the ground.

If $d = 125$ metres when $t = 5$ seconds, work out:

a) The constant of proportionality.

Answer _____ [2]

b) The time taken for the apple to fall 48 metres. Give your answer to 1 decimal place.

Answer _____ [2]

Total Marks _____ / 10

Variation and Compound Measures

1 £4000 is invested at 1.6% compound interest per annum.

Work out its value after three years. Give your answer to the nearest pound.

Answer _____ [3]

2 A greyhound runs 77.8 metres in eight seconds. What is the greyhound's average speed in:

a) Metres per second (to 3 decimal places)?

Answer _____ [2]

b) Kilometres per hour (to 2 decimal places)?

Answer _____ [2]

3 A silver ring weighing 2g has a density of 10.49g/cm³.

Work out the volume of silver in the ring.
Give your answer to an appropriate degree of accuracy.

Answer _____ [2]

4 The force (F) between two magnets is inversely proportional to the square of the distance (d) between them.

Work out the constant of proportionality if $F = 12$ when $d = 3$.

Answer _____ [3]

Total Marks _____ / 12

Angles and Shapes 1 & 2

1 Work out the value of x. 🖩

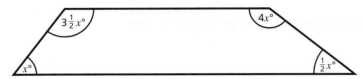

Answer _____ [2]

2 The interior angle of a regular polygon is 150°.

Work out how many sides the polygon has. 🖩

Answer _____ [2]

3 A helicopter leaves its base and flies 40km on a bearing of 050° and then 30km on a bearing of 105°. 🖩

a) Draw a scale diagram to show this information. How far is the helicopter from its base?

Answer _____ [2]

b) On what bearing does the helicopter need to fly in order to return to its base?

Answer _____ [1]

Total Marks _____ / 7

Fractions

1 Which of these fractions is equivalent to $\frac{5}{7}$?

Circle your answer.

$\frac{35}{45}$ $\frac{45}{63}$ $\frac{25}{40}$ $\frac{15}{22}$ **[1]**

2 Neesha ate $\frac{2}{3}$ of her chocolate bar this morning and then ate $\frac{3}{5}$ of what was left in the afternoon. How much is left to eat tomorrow?

Answer _____ **[2]**

3 Which is larger, $\frac{7}{9}$ of 81 or $\frac{2}{7}$ of 217? You must show your working.

Answer _____ **[2]**

4 Express 14 minutes as a fraction of 2.4 hours. Give your answer in the simplest form.

Answer _____ **[2]**

5 Change $0.2\dot{7}$ to a fraction in its simplest form.

Answer _____ **[3]**

6 Find the value of p if $\left(\frac{3}{2}\right)^{p} - \frac{3}{2} = \frac{3}{4}$

Answer _____ **[2]**

Total Marks _____ / 12

Percentages

1 In five months, a population of rats increases in number by 20% and then by 35%.

If there were 150 rats originally, how many are there at the end of the five-month period?

Answer _____ [2]

2 Write down 18g as a percentage of 0.075kg.

Answer _____ [2]

3 In a small village school, 22% of the children caught chicken pox.

If 11 children caught chicken pox, how many children attended the school?

Answer _____ [2]

4 This year, Pratik grew 31 tomato plants. This is a 38% reduction on last year.

How many tomato plants did Pratik grow last year?

Answer _____ [2]

5 Temi paid tax on £14000 at 24%. She paid the tax in 12 equal monthly instalments.
Circle the payment she made each month.

£336   £48.61   £280   £70   [1]

Total Marks _____ / 9

Probability 1 & 2

1   A spinner has five sides: red, blue, yellow, green and pink.

The table below shows the probability associated with each colour.

Colour	Red	Blue	Yellow	Green	Pink
Probability	x	0.3	x	$3x$	0.2

a) Find the value of x.

Answer _____ [3]

b) Is the spinner fair? Give a reason for your answer.

_____ [2]

2   A bag contains n counters. Five of the counters are blue, three are yellow and the rest are red.

A counter is taken from the bag at random.

a) Write an expression in terms of n to represent the probability that the counter is red.

Answer _____ [2]

b) The counter is replaced and two counters are taken from the bag at random.

Show that the probability that one counter is blue and the other is yellow is $\dfrac{30}{n(n-1)}$

_____ [2]

3 A veterinary practice surveyed its clients to find out what pets they owned.

95 clients took part. 75 clients owned a cat (C), 30 clients owned a rabbit (R) and 15 owned both.

a) Complete the Venn diagram to show this information. [1]

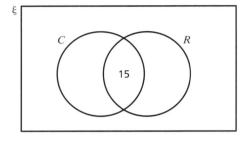

b) Write down the probability that a client owns neither a cat nor a rabbit.

Answer _____ [2]

4 A biased dice has five faces numbered 1 to 5.

The probability the dice lands on a 5 is 0.18

The dice is rolled twice and the score recorded.

a) Complete the probability tree diagram. [2]
   5' means 'not 5'.

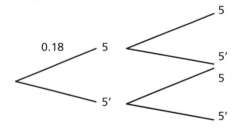

b) Calculate the probability that the dice lands on a 5 on only one of the two rolls.

Answer _____ [3]

Total Marks _____ / 17

Number Patterns and Sequences & Terms and Rules

1 Here are the first three terms in a sequence of numbers:

8, 5, 2, ___, ___

a) Write down the next two terms in the sequence.

Answer _____ [2]

b) Work out the expression for the nth term of the sequence. Circle your answer.

$11 - 3n$ $3n + 5$ $-3n + 5$ $3n + 11$ [1]

c) Jennifer thinks that −15 is a number in this sequence.

Is Jennifer correct? Explain your answer.

_____ [2]

2 The following numbers form a geometric sequence.

3, 6, 12, 24, ___, ___

a) Write down the next two terms in the sequence.

Answer _____ [1]

b) The sequence can be represented by a recursive relationship.
Circle the correct formula below.

$U_{n+1} = 2U_n$ $U_{n+1} = U_n + 3$ $U_{n+1} = (U_n)^3$ $3U_{n+1} = U_n$ [1]

3 Work out the next term in this cubic sequence.

3, 17, 55, 129 …

Answer _____ [1]

4 Write down the first five terms in the sequence $3^n + 2$.

Answer _____ [2]

Total Marks _____ / 10

Transformations

1

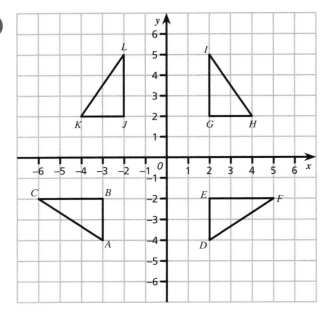

Describe the single transformation that maps:

a) Triangle *ABC* onto triangle *DEF*.

_____

_____ [2]

b) Triangle *DEF* onto triangle *GHI*.

_____

_____ [3]

c) Triangle *DEF* onto triangle *JKL*.

_____

_____ [2]

2 On the grid below plot the points: *A*(2, 1), *B*(4, 1) and *C*(3, 5). Join the points together. Using construction lines, enlarge triangle *ABC* by scale factor 2, centre of enlargement (0, 0), to form triangle *DEF*.

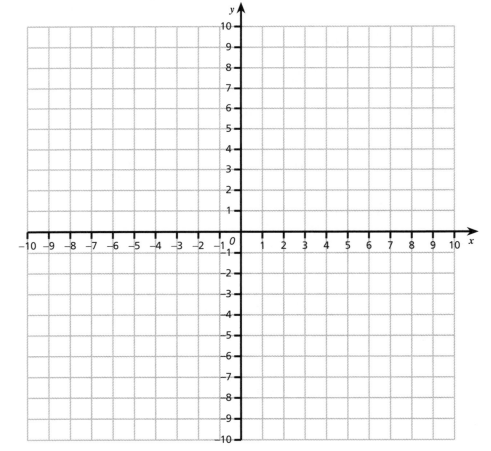

[3]

Total Marks _____ / 10

Constructions

1 Using a pair of compasses and a ruler, mark two points, C and D, that are 5cm apart.

Draw the locus of points that are equidistant from C and D.

[2]

2 Draw any triangle ABC.

Construct the bisectors of each angle using a pair of compasses and a ruler.

[3]

3 A pyramid has a rectangular base 3cm by 4cm and a height of 5cm.

Draw an accurate plan view of the pyramid.

[2]

Linear Graphs

1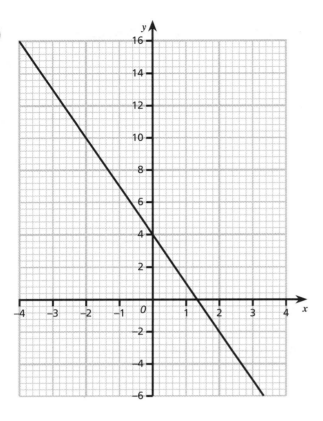

Work out the equation of the line shown.

Answer _____ [3]

2 A line has the equation $5y + 2x = 7$

Work out the gradient of the line. Circle your answer.

$\frac{2}{5}$ 2 $-\frac{2}{5}$ $-\frac{5}{2}$ [1]

3 Work out the equation of the line that goes through points (1, 5) and (6, 15).

Answer _____ [3]

4 A graph crosses the y-axis at the point (0, 5) and the x-axis at the point (5, 0).

Write down the equation of the line in the form $ax + by + c = 0$, where
a, b and c are integers.

Answer _____ [2]

Total Marks _____ / 9

Graphs of Quadratic Functions

1 A graph has the equation $y = 2x^2 - 7$

a) Complete the table below.

x	−2	−1	0	1	2
y					

[1]

b) Plot the graph of the equation on the axes below.

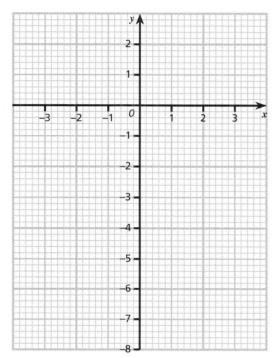

[2]

2 The graph of $y = f(x)$ is shown below.

The maximum is the point (−0.5, 0.5)

The minimum is the point (0.75, −1.5)

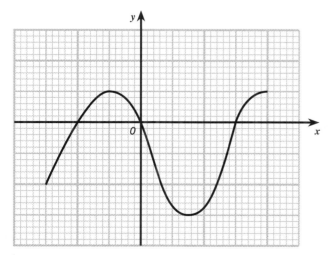

Write down the coordinates of the maximum and minimum points for the graphs of the following equations:

a) $f(x + 2)$

Maximum: _____

Minimum: _____ [2]

b) $-f(x)$

Maximum: _____

Minimum: _____ [2]

Total Marks _____ / 7

Powers, Roots and Indices

1 $\sqrt{8} + 2\sqrt{2} = k\sqrt{2}$

Work out the value of k. Circle your answer.

      6   4   10   5   [1]

2 Simplify $(2x^2 y)^3$

Answer _____ [2]

3 Work out the value of $\left(\frac{9}{64}\right)^{\frac{1}{2}}$. Circle your answer.

      $\frac{9}{32}$ $\frac{3}{8}$ $\frac{3}{64}$ $\frac{3}{32}$

                                                            [1]

4 Rationalise $\dfrac{\sqrt{3} - 1}{\sqrt{3}}$

Answer _____ [2]

5 Work out the area of the rectangle. Give your answer in the form $a - b\sqrt{3}$.

$\sqrt{3}$

$\sqrt{3} - 2$

Answer _____ [2]

Total Marks _____ / 8

Area and Volume 1 & 2

1 The diagram below is the cross-section of a swimming pool.

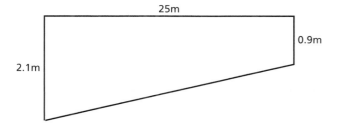

The swimming pool is 10m wide. The pool fills at a rate of 0.2m³ per second.

How many hours does it take to fill the pool completely?

Give your answer to 3 significant figures.

Answer _____ [4]

2 The ratio of the radius to the height of a cylinder is 1 : 3
The volume of the cylinder is 275πcm³.

Calculate the value of the radius. Give your answer to 3 significant figures.

Answer _____ [4]

Total Marks _____ / 8

Uses of Graphs

1 x is inversely proportional to y.

Which graph represents this relationship? Tick a box.

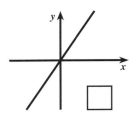 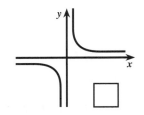 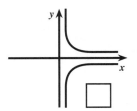 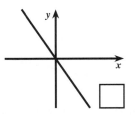

[1]

2 A line has the equation $2y = 3x + 5$

Work out the equation of the line that is perpendicular to it and goes through point (3, 6).

Answer _____ [4]

3 The formula $C = 3M + 2$ represents how the cost of a phone call is calculated by a telephone company, where C is the cost in pence and M is the number of minutes.

Write down the gradient of the line and use it to describe the rate of change.

[2]

Total Marks _____ / 7

Other Graphs 1

1 The graph below shows the journey of a car.

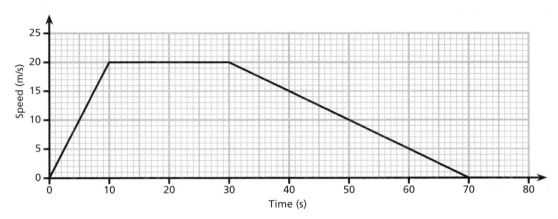

Speed (m/s) vs Time (s)

a) Describe the journey of the car.

_____

_____

_____ [3]

b) Calculate the distance covered by the car.

Answer _____ [3]

2 Sketch the graph of $y = x^3 - 1$ and label the y-intercept.

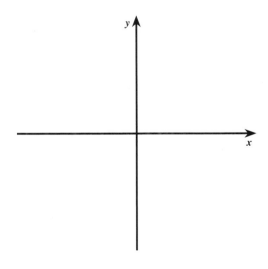

[2]

Total Marks _____ / 8

Other Graphs 2

1 A circle has the equation $x^2 + y^2 = 45$

Circle the correct value for the radius.

$r = 45$ $r = \dfrac{45}{2}$ $r = 3\sqrt{5}$ $r = 7$ [1]

2 A ball is thrown up in the air. The speed of the ball over the first three seconds is shown in the graph below.

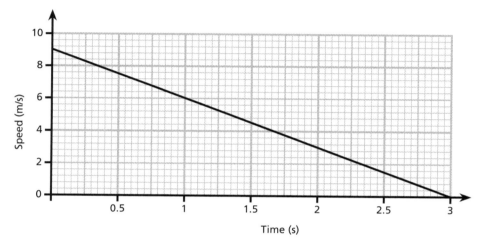

a) Write down the initial speed of the ball.

Answer _____ [1]

b) Explain what happens to the ball at three seconds.

_____ [1]

c) Work out the distance travelled by the ball in the three-second period.

Answer _____ [2]

3 A circle has the equation $x^2 + y^2 = 58$

Work out the equation of the tangent that meets the circle at point (3, 7).

Answer _____ [4]

Total Marks _____ / 9

Inequalities

1 If $-6 \leqslant d \leqslant 2$ and $-5 \leqslant e \leqslant 5$, work out:

a) The largest possible value of $d \times e$.

Answer _____ [1]

b) The smallest possible value of $d \times e$.

Answer _____ [1]

2 Work out the values of y that satisfy these two inequalities:

$2y > -12$ and $3y + 4 \leqslant 19$

[3]

3 On the grid, plot the graphs of $x = 0$, $x + y = 10$ and $y = x$.

Shade the region that represents the inequalities $x \geqslant 0$, $x + y \leqslant 10$ and $y \geqslant x$.

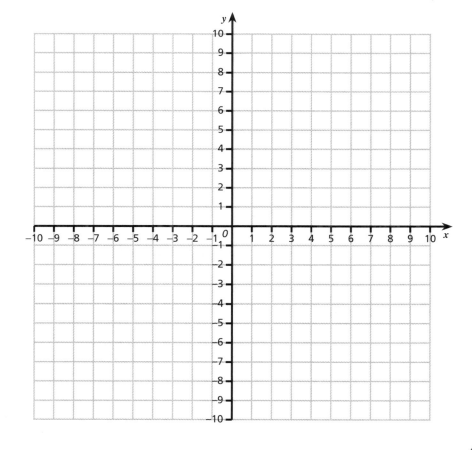

[4]

Congruence and Geometrical Problems

1 Here are four triangles, A, B, C and D.

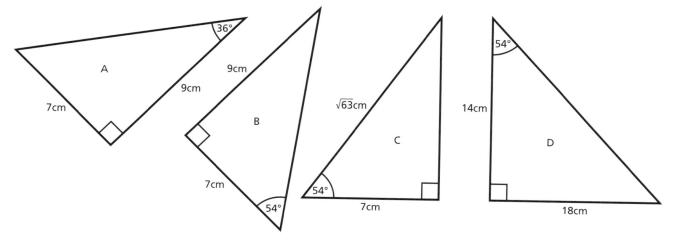

a) Which two triangles are congruent? Give a reason for your answer.

Answer _____ [2]

b) Which triangles are similar to triangle A?

Answer _____ [1]

2 A man who is 1.6m tall is standing by a lamp post. He casts a shadow that is 2.8m long.

Work out the height of a lamp post that casts a shadow 38m long.
Give your answer to 1 decimal place.

Answer _____ [2]

3 Two mugs, A and B, are similar. Mug A has a height of 10cm and mug B has a height of 8cm.
Mug A has a volume of 36cm³.

Work out the volume of mug B to the nearest cm³.

Answer _____ [3]

Total Marks _____ / 8

Right-Angled Triangles

1 The diagonal of a square has a length of 16cm.

Calculate the square's side length to 2 decimal places.

Answer _____ [3]

2 A cuboid box has a length of 13cm, a width of 12cm and a height of 5cm.

Is it possible to fit a pencil of length 18cm into the box? You **must** show your working.

[3]

3 From the top of a lookout tower of height 20m, a lifeguard sees two boats.

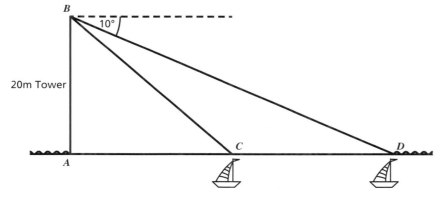

If the angles of depression of the two boats are 10° and 29°, calculate the distance between the two boats. Give your answer to the nearest metre.

Answer _____ [3]

Total Marks _____ / 9

Sine and Cosine Rules

1. Two bees, Buzz and Hum, leave a hive simultaneously.
   Buzz flies 32m due south and Hum flies 19m on a bearing of 133°.

   a) How far apart are the two bees? Give your answer to 2 decimal places.

   Answer _____ [3]

   b) What is the area of the region enclosed by the hive, Hum and Buzz?
      Give your answer to the nearest square metre.

   Answer _____ [2]

   c) Hum flies at 40 centimetres per second. How long will it take Hum to reach Buzz?

   Answer _____ [2]

2. The forensic police rope off a triangular plot of ground DEF.
   $DE = 30.4$m and $DF = 32$m.

   If angle $FDE = 52°$ and angle $DEF = 67°$, calculate the length of rope needed by the
   police to cordon off the area. Give your answer to 1 decimal place.

   Answer _____ [3]

   Total Marks _____ / 10

Statistics 1

1 The scatter diagram below shows the total time spent studying and the mark obtained in a mathematics test for 11 students.

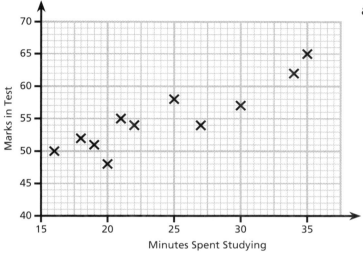

a) Another student took the test. They spent 15 minutes studying and scored 46 marks.

Add this student to the scatter diagram. [1]

b) Write down the type of correlation shown by the graph.

Answer _____ [1]

c) Explain what this correlation might mean.

_____ [1]

d) Draw a line of best fit. [1]

e) Use your line of best fit to estimate the time spent studying by a student who scored a mark of 60 in the test.

Answer _____ [1]

2 Rebecca calculates the mean time taken for her class to run 100m.
She calculates a mean of 15.2 seconds for her 23 classmates, but realises she has accidentally used a time of 21.3 instead of 12.3

Correct the mean time taken.

Answer _____ [3]

Total Marks _____ / 8

Statistics 2

1 The cumulative frequency curve below shows the length of 36 leaves taken from a tree.

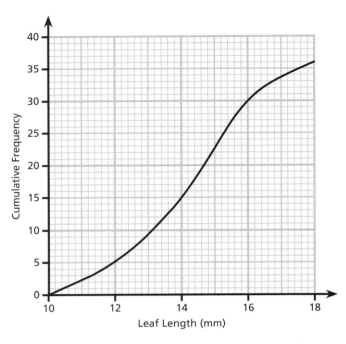

a) Use the curve to estimate the median leaf length.

Answer _____ [1]

b) Use the curve to find an estimate for the interquartile range.

Answer _____ [1]

c) Draw a box plot to represent this data.

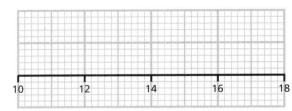

[3]

d) The box plot below shows the data from another tree.
Compare the length of leaves on the two trees.

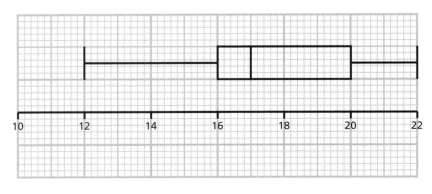

_____

_____ [2]

Total Marks _____ / 7

Measures, Accuracy and Finance

1 Estimate the value of (8.64 × 0.864) ÷ (8.4 − 8)

Answer _____ [2]

2 Members of the Crawshaw family enjoy camping holidays and often take their car to France by ferry. The ferry prices for a two-way trip are: cars £46, plus £12.50 per adult and £8.70 per child.

The campsite has a daily charge of €12.50 for cars, €10 per adult and €5 per child. The rate of exchange is €1 = £0.78

Calculate the total cost in pounds for the two parents and two children in the Crawshaw family to:

a) Make a single ferry crossing.

Answer _____ [2]

b) Stay for three days at the French campsite.

Answer _____ [2]

3 Find the largest and smallest possible areas of a rectangle that measures 6 cm by 7 cm, where each length is correct to the nearest centimetre.

Largest area = _____ cm² [1]

Smallest area = _____ cm² [1]

Total Marks _____ / 8

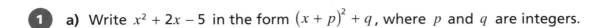

1 **a)** Write $x^2 + 2x - 5$ in the form $(x + p)^2 + q$, where p and q are integers.

Answer _____ [2]

b) Use your answer to part **a)** to solve the equation $x^2 + 2x - 5 = 0$
Give your answers in surd form.

Answer _____ [2]

c) Write down the coordinates of the turning point of $x^2 + 2x - 5$.

Answer _____ [1]

2 A square has side length $x + 3$ cm. The numerical value for the area of the square is equal to that of the perimeter.

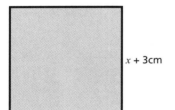

$x + 3$ cm

a) Show that $x^2 + 2x - 3 = 0$

[4]

b) Work out the side length of the square.

Answer _____ [2]

Total Marks _____ / 11

Simultaneous Equations and Functions

1 Solve the simultaneous equations:

$x^2 + y^2 = 10$

$y = x + 2$

Answer _____ [4]

2 $f(x) = 3x + 5$

$g(x) = x^2 - 2x$

a) Work out the value of $f(3)$

Answer _____ [1]

b) Work out $gf(x)$

Answer _____ [2]

c) Solve $gf(x) = 0$

Answer _____ [2]

Total Marks _____ / 9

Algebraic Proof

1 Show that $(2a - 1)^2 - (2b - 1)^2 = 4(a - b)(a + b - 1)$

[4]

2 Prove that the difference between the squares of any two consecutive odd numbers is a multiple of 8.

[4]

3 Show that $0.888\,888\,88\ldots$ can be written as $\frac{8}{9}$.

[4]

Circles

1 Work out the size of angle BAE. Give a reason for your answer.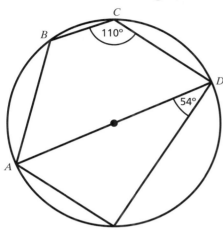

Answer _____ [3]

2 Work out the value of d.

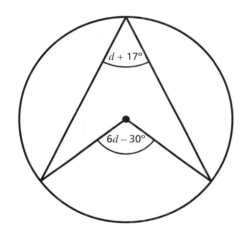

Answer _____ [2]

3 Calculate the size of angles a, b, and c.

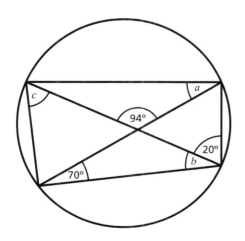

$a =$ _____ [1]

$b =$ _____ [1]

$c =$ _____ [1]

Vectors

1 Here are five vectors:

$\overrightarrow{KL}$ = 4**p** + 8**q**, $\overrightarrow{MN}$ = 8**p** + 16**q**, $\overrightarrow{OP}$ = –4**p** + 8**q**, $\overrightarrow{QR}$ = 12**p** – 24**q**

and $\overrightarrow{ST}$ = 12**p** + 24**q**

Which vectors are parallel?

Answer _____ [3]

2 $ABCD$ is a kite. The diagonals BD and AC intersect at E.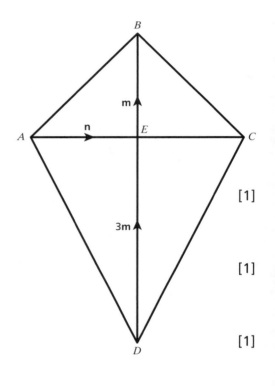

$\overrightarrow{AE}$ = **n**, $\overrightarrow{DE}$ = 3**m**, $\overrightarrow{EB}$ = **m**

Work out the vector expressions for:

a) $\overrightarrow{DB}$

Answer _____ [1]

b) $\overrightarrow{CA}$

Answer _____ [1]

c) $\overrightarrow{DA}$

Answer _____ [1]

d) $\overrightarrow{AB}$

Answer _____ [1]

3 $ABCD$ is a quadrilateral where $\overrightarrow{AB}$ = **a**, $\overrightarrow{BC}$ = **b**, $\overrightarrow{CD}$ = **c** and $\overrightarrow{AD}$ = 2**b**

Name the type of quadrilateral.

Answer _____ [1]

Total Marks _____ / 8

Collins

GCSE
Mathematics
Paper 1 Higher tier

H

Materials

Time allowed: 1 hour 30 minutes

For this paper you must have:

- mathematical instruments

You may **not** use a calculator.

Instructions

- Use black ink or black ball-point pen. Draw diagrams in pencil.
- Answer **all** questions.
- You must answer the questions in the space provided.
- In all calculations, show clearly how you work out your answer.

Information

- The marks for questions are shown in brackets.
- The maximum mark for this paper is 80.

Name: ....

Practice Exam Paper 1

1 Circle the formula for calculating pressure, where F = Force, A = Area and D = Density.

$P = \dfrac{F}{A}$ $\qquad\qquad$ $P = \dfrac{D}{F}$ $\qquad\qquad$ $P = \dfrac{A}{F}$ $\qquad\qquad$ $P = \dfrac{A}{D}$ $\qquad$ **[1 mark]**

2 What is the value of sin 30°?

Circle your answer.

1 $\qquad\qquad\qquad$ $\sqrt{\dfrac{3}{2}}$ $\qquad\qquad\qquad$ $\dfrac{1}{2}$ $\qquad\qquad\qquad$ $\dfrac{1}{\sqrt{3}}$ $\qquad$ **[1 mark]**

3 Expand $(x + 1)(x + 2)(x + 3)$

Circle your answer.

$x^3 + 6x^2 + 8x + 6$ $\qquad$ $x^3 + 6x^2 + 11x + 6$ $\qquad$ $x^3 + 6x + 6$ $\qquad$ $x^2 + 3x + 2$ $\qquad$ **[1 mark]**

4 Here is a sequence: $\qquad$ 1 $\quad$ 4 $\quad$ 9 $\quad$ 16 $\quad$ 25

Circle the expression for the nth term of the sequence.

$n + 3$ $\qquad\qquad$ $3n - 2$ $\qquad\qquad$ $n + 5$ $\qquad\qquad$ n^2 $\qquad$ **[1 mark]**

5   **(a)** What is one million minus one?

Answer _____ **[1 mark]**

(b) 3, 12, 15, 25, 27, 60

From the numbers above choose:

(i)   the cube number   Answer _____

(ii) the square number   Answer _____

(iii) the LCM of 12 and 15.   Answer _____ **[3 marks]**

(c) Sandra says,

"If I double a prime number and then add three, the answer will always be a prime."

Give two prime numbers for which this statement is true and two prime numbers for which this statement is **not** true (do not use 2 or 3).

True: _____ and _____

Not True: _____ and _____ **[2 marks]**

6   Work out 1.8444 ÷ 1.2

Answer _____ **[2 marks]**

TURN OVER FOR THE NEXT QUESTION

7 **(a)** If $a = \frac{1}{2}$, $b = \frac{1}{4}$ and $c = -\frac{1}{8}$, work out the value of $a^2b - c$

Answer _____ **[2 marks]**

(b) Solve the equation $\frac{(m + 3)}{m} = 2$

Answer _____ **[1 mark]**

(c) $16^p = 4^4$

Work out the value of p.

Answer _____ **[1 mark]**

8

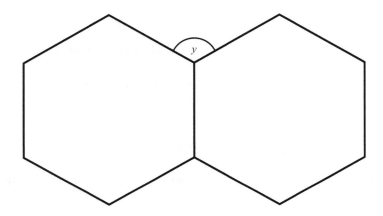

The diagram shows two regular hexagons.

Work out the size of angle y.

You **must** show your working.

Answer _____ **[4 marks]**

9

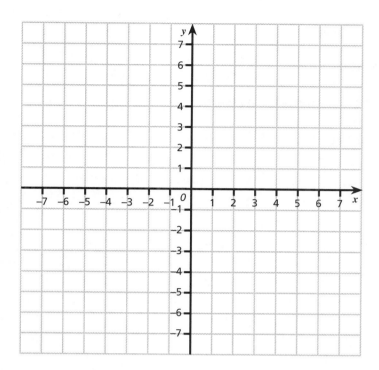

(a) On the grid draw triangle A with vertices (–3, 0), (–3, 3) and (–1, 3). [2 marks]

(b) Reflect triangle A in $x = 0$ to form triangle B. [2 marks]

(c) Rotate triangle B clockwise 90° about the origin. Label the image C. [2 marks]

(d) What transformation maps triangle A onto triangle C?

_____ [2 marks]

TURN OVER FOR THE NEXT QUESTION

10 Two men invest £8000 and £6000 into a business.

In the first year, the business makes a profit of £1064.

The profit is divided in the ratio of the original amounts invested.

Work out the value of each share of the profit.

Answer _____ [4 marks]

11 Tick whether each statement is **true** or **false**.

	TRUE	FALSE	
(a) A parallelogram has rotational symmetry of order 2.	☐	☐	[1 mark]
(b) A rhombus has rotational symmetry of order 4.	☐	☐	[1 mark]
(c) A hexagon can be drawn with only one line of symmetry.	☐	☐	[2 marks]
(d) An isosceles triangle with more than one line of symmetry is an equilateral triangle.	☐	☐	[2 marks]

12 **(a)** Estimate the answer to $\frac{(51.7 \times 112.1)}{(81.7 + 15.9)}$

Answer _____ [2 marks]

(b) If $x = 3.2 \times 10^4$ and $y = 2.3 \times 10^5$, work out the value of $x + y$ in standard form.

Answer _____ [2 marks]

(c) Write 0.0006812 correct to 3 significant figures.

Answer _____ [1 mark]

(d) Work out $5 + 4 \times 3 - 14 \div 2$

Answer _____ [1 mark]

TURN OVER FOR THE NEXT QUESTION

13 **(a)** Draw the graph of $y = x^2 - 4x + 1$ using values of x from -1 to 5.　　　　**[2 marks]**

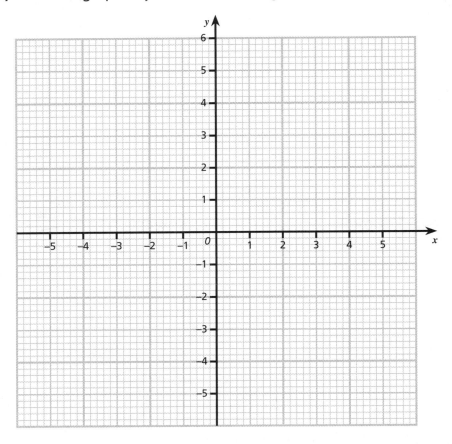

(b) Use your graph to solve $x^2 - 4x + 1 = 0$

Answer _____ **[2 marks]**

(c) Work out the equation of the line of symmetry for $y = x^2 - 4x + 1$

Answer _____ **[2 marks]**

14   **(a)** Simplify $y^2 + y^2 + y^2$

Answer _____ **[1 mark]**

(b) Expand $4 - 2m(m + 3)$

Answer _____ **[2 marks]**

(c) Expand and fully factorise $p(p - t) + t(p - t)$

Answer _____ **[2 marks]**

(d) Expand and simplify $(3a + 2)(a - 4)$

Answer _____ **[2 marks]**

TURN OVER FOR THE NEXT QUESTION

15 A bag contains eight marbles. Two marbles are yellow and six marbles are blue.

A marble is selected and not replaced.

A second marble is selected.

What is the probability of obtaining:

(a) Two yellow marbles?

Answer _____ **[3 marks]**

(b) One marble that is yellow and one marble that is blue?

Answer _____ **[3 marks]**

16   Write down the value of:

(a) 14^0

Answer _____ **[1 mark]**

(b) $64^{\frac{1}{2}}$

Answer _____ **[1 mark]**

(c) 7^{-1}

Answer _____ **[1 mark]**

(d) $\left(\frac{1}{8}\right)^{-1}$

Answer _____ **[1 mark]**

(e) $(0.1)^{-3}$

Answer _____ **[2 marks]**

TURN OVER FOR THE NEXT QUESTION

17 The owner of an aquarium likes to regularly measure the length (y) of all his fish that are smaller than one metre.

The lengths of 100 fish are shown below.

Length (cm)	Frequency	Cumulative Frequency
$0 \leqslant y < 10$	6	
$10 \leqslant y < 20$	4	
$20 \leqslant y < 30$	9	
$30 \leqslant y < 40$	10	
$40 \leqslant y < 50$	13	
$50 \leqslant y < 60$	18	
$60 \leqslant y < 70$	14	
$70 \leqslant y < 80$	14	
$80 \leqslant y < 90$	7	
$90 \leqslant y < 100$	5	

(a) Complete the cumulative frequency column in the table.   **[2 marks]**

(b) Plot a cumulative frequency curve for this data.

[2 marks]

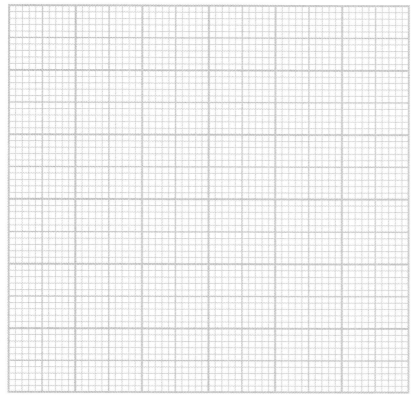

(c) Estimate the median length of the 100 fish.

Answer _____ [1 mark]

(d) Estimate the interquartile range.

Answer _____ [2 marks]

TURN OVER FOR THE NEXT QUESTION

18   Write down as a fraction in its lowest terms:

$$\frac{1}{a + 2} + \frac{a}{a^2 + 6a + 8}$$

Answer _____ **[4 marks]**

END OF QUESTIONS

GCSE
Mathematics
Paper 2 Higher tier

H

Materials

Time allowed: 1 hour 30 minutes

For this paper you must have:

- a calculator
- mathematical instruments.

Instructions

- Use black ink or black ball-point pen. Draw diagrams in pencil.
- Answer **all** questions.
- You must answer the questions in the space provided.
- In all calculations, show clearly how you work out your answer.

Information

- The marks for questions are shown in brackets.
- The maximum mark for this paper is 80.

Name: ....

Practice Exam Paper 2

1 What is the value of $3000 \times 70\,000$ in standard form?

Circle your answer.

210 000 000 21×10^7 2.1×10^8 2.1×10^9 **[1 mark]**

2 Work out y if $2^{y+2} = 8^{y-2}$

Circle your answer.

6   4   2   0   **[1 mark]**

3 The formula $d + \dfrac{m}{p} = c$ is rearranged to make m the subject.

What is m?

Circle your answer.

$pc - d$ $p(c - d)$ $\dfrac{(c - d)}{p}$ $pc + pd$ **[1 mark]**

4 What is the value of 5365.255 correct to 2 significant figures?

Circle your answer.

5365.26   5365.25   5400   54   **[1 mark]**

5   Use your calculator to work out $(5.6 + 2.1)^2 \times 1.03$

(a) Write down all the figures on your calculator.

Answer _____ **[1 mark]**

(b) Write down the answer to 2 decimal places.

Answer _____ **[1 mark]**

6   A cast iron rod has a mass of 270kg.

(a) If its density is 7.5g/cm³, calculate the volume of the rod.

Answer _____ cm³   **[2 marks]**

(b) If the cross-sectional area of the rod is 12cm², calculate the length of the rod in metres.

Answer _____ m   **[2 marks]**

TURN OVER FOR THE NEXT QUESTION

7   A helicopter leaves Biggin Hill airport and flies 40km due north.

It then flies 15km due west.

Calculate:

(a) The shortest distance the helicopter has to fly to return to Biggin Hill airport.

Write your answer correct to 2 decimal places.

Answer _____   [3 marks]

(b) The bearing that the helicopter will need to fly to return to Biggin Hill airport.

Give your answer to the nearest degree.

Answer _____   [3 marks]

8 In the space below, use a pair of compasses, a ruler and pencil to construct an equilateral triangle with sides of length 8cm.

You must show all construction lines.

[2 marks]

9 Solve these simultaneous equations:

$5x - 2y = 8$

$7x + 3y = 17$

$x =$ _____

$y =$ _____ [4 marks]

TURN OVER FOR THE NEXT QUESTION

10 A rectangular swimming pool has internal dimensions of:

width 14m; length 24m; a constant depth of 1.4m

It is made from concrete and the walls and base of the pool are 10cm thick.

(a) Work out the capacity of the swimming pool in litres, if 1000cm³ = 1 litre.

Answer _____ **[2 marks]**

(b) Water is pumped into the pool at a rate of 2 litres per second.

How long would it take to fill the swimming pool? Give your answer to the nearest hour.

Answer _____ **[3 marks]**

(c) Work out the volume of concrete that would be needed to make the swimming pool.

Give your answer in cubic metres.

Answer _____ m³ **[3 marks]**

11 On 7th May 1954, Roger Bannister became the first person to run a mile in 3 minutes 59 seconds.

Assuming 5 miles = 8 kilometres, calculate his average speed in kilometres per hour.

Answer _____ [4 marks]

12 **(a)** Solve $14 - 2m = m + 12$

Answer _____ [2 marks]

(b) $p = \frac{1}{2}q + 1$

Rearrange the formula to make q the subject.

Answer _____ [2 marks]

TURN OVER FOR THE NEXT QUESTION

13 The diagram represents the ground floor of Denis and Theresa's house.

All measurements are in metres.

The kitchen is a square of side length x.

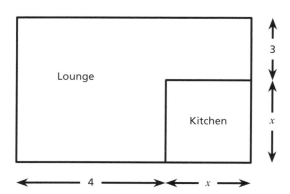

(a) Write down an expression for the perimeter of the ground floor.

Answer _____ [2 marks]

(b) The perimeter of the ground floor is 24 metres.

Calculate the area of the lounge.

Answer _____ [2 marks]

(c) Carpet costs £24 per square metre. In a sale it is reduced by 12%.

Denis and Theresa have put aside £625 to carpet the lounge.

Is this enough money?

You **must** show all your working.

[3 marks]

14 Cans of soup have a radius of 5cm and a height of 10cm.

The cans are packed into a box in two layers, with five rows of six cans on each layer.

Each can costs 24p to make and is sold for 45p.

Calculate:

(a) The percentage profit made on each can of soup.

Answer _____ **[2 marks]**

(b) The total surface area of one can of soup (take π as 3.142).

Answer _____ **[4 marks]**

(c) The cost of aluminium used to make the cans in one box, to the nearest penny, if the price of aluminium is 20p per square metre.

Answer _____ **[4 marks]**

TURN OVER FOR THE NEXT QUESTION

15 Here are two circles with centre points C and G.

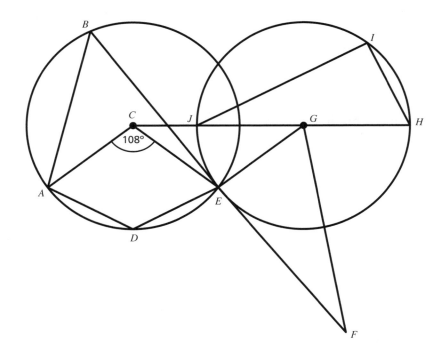

Work out the size of:

(a) Angle ABE.

Answer _____ **[1 mark]**

(b) Angle GEF.

Answer _____ **[1 mark]**

(c) Angle HIJ.

Answer _____ **[1 mark]**

(d) Angle ADE.

Answer _____ **[1 mark]**

16   Work out the compound interest earned on £3000 invested for six years at 2% per annum.

Answer _____ **[4 marks]**

17   Solve the quadratic equation $x^2 - 5x + 3 = 0$

Give your solutions correct to 3 significant figures.

Answer _____ **[4 marks]**

TURN OVER FOR THE NEXT QUESTION

18   Adrian walks from his home (A) on a bearing of 060° for 1.6km until he reaches Harvey's home (H).

At H he turns on a bearing of 280° and travels a further 4.8km to the guitar shop (G).

He then returns directly home.

How far does Adrian have to walk from the guitar shop to his home?

Give your answer to 3 decimal places.

Answer _____   **[4 marks]**

19 A stone is dropped h metres from a cliff.

The value of h is directly proportional to the square of the time (t).

When $t = 4$ seconds, $h = 8$ metres.

Calculate the value of h when $t = 16$ seconds.

Answer _____ **[3 marks]**

20 A line has the equation $y = 4x + 6$

Find the equation of the line that is perpendicular to it and that passes through the point (0, 4).

Answer _____ **[3 marks]**

TURN OVER FOR THE NEXT QUESTION

21 The lengths of the sides of a rectangle are $12 + \sqrt{7}$ and $12 - \sqrt{7}$ units.

Work out in the simplest form:

(a) The perimeter of the rectangle.

Answer _____ [1 mark]

(b) The area of the rectangle.

Answer _____ [2 marks]

END OF QUESTIONS

Collins

GCSE
Mathematics
Paper 3 Higher tier

H

Materials

Time allowed: 1 hour 30 minutes

For this paper you must have:

- a calculator
- mathematical instruments.

Instructions

- Use black ink or black ball-point pen. Draw diagrams in pencil.
- Answer **all** questions.
- You must answer the questions in the space provided.
- In all calculations, show clearly how you work out your answer.

Information

- The marks for questions are shown in brackets.
- The maximum mark for this paper is 80.

Name: ....

Practice Exam Paper 3

1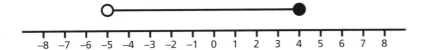

Circle the inequality shown on this diagram.

$-5 \leqslant x \leqslant 4$ $-5 \leqslant x < 4$ $-5 < x < 4$ $-5 < x \leqslant 4$ **[1 mark]**

2 Circle the fraction that is equivalent to $5\frac{4}{6}$ in its simplest form.

$\frac{9}{6}$ $\frac{20}{6}$ $\frac{10}{3}$ $\frac{17}{3}$ **[1 mark]**

3 How many faces does a hexagonal-based pyramid have?

Circle your answer.

5   6   7   8   **[1 mark]**

4 Circle the roots of the graph produced by the equation $x^2 - 5x + 6$.

2 and 3   −2 and −3   1 and 6   −1 and −6   **[1 mark]**

5   Work out $3(x + 2) = 4(x - 5)$

Answer _____ [2 marks]

6   Fully factorise $4y^2 - 16y$

Answer _____ [2 marks]

7   The ratio of the number of boys to girls in a football club was 6 : 1

The club ran a campaign to encourage more girls to join.

Eight more girls joined the club and the ratio of boys to girls changed to 4 : 1

How many boys are members of the club?

Answer _____ [3 marks]

TURN OVER FOR THE NEXT QUESTION

8 The diagram shows a square.

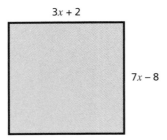

$3x + 2$

$7x - 8$

Work out the value of x.

Answer _____ **[3 marks]**

9

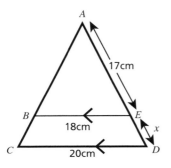

Work out the value of x.

Answer _____ **[3 marks]**

10

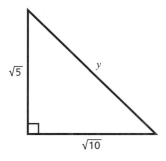

Work out the value of *y*.

Answer _____ [3 marks]

11 A company is employing temporary workers.

It calls 20 people in for an interview.

Out of the 20 candidates three have a HGV licence.

The company hires three employees from those interviewed.

What is the probability that:

(a) All three have a HGV licence?

Answer _____ [2 marks]

(b) Only one has a HGV licence?

Answer _____ [3 marks]

TURN OVER FOR THE NEXT QUESTION

12 A three-sided spinner coloured red, blue and yellow is spun 100 times. The results are recorded:

Colour	Red	Blue	Yellow
Frequency	42	27	31

The spinner is spun again.

(a) Estimate the probability that the spinner lands on blue.

Answer _____ **[1 mark]**

(b) The spinner is spun a further 600 times.

Estimate the number of times the spinner will land on yellow.

Answer _____ **[2 marks]**

13 On the diagram $\overrightarrow{OA} = $ **a**, $\overrightarrow{OB} = $ **b** and $\overrightarrow{OC} = 3$**b** $- 2$**a**.

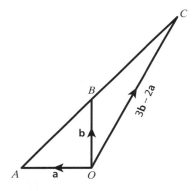

Prove that ABC is a straight line.

Answer _____ **[3 marks]**

14 Calculate the volume of the pyramid.

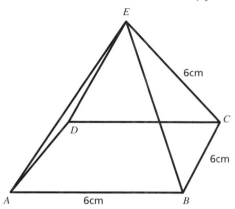

Answer _____ **[4 marks]**

15 A flower pot company has two customer services operatives who deal with telephone enquiries.

The following table shows data on the length of telephone calls received in one day:

	Shortest Time	Lowest Quartile	Median Time	Upper Quartile	Longest Time
Bill	1m 10s	2m 20s	3m 30s	4m 50s	7m 10s
Ben	40s	2m 20s	5m 10s	7m 30s	10m 45s

(a) Draw two box plots to compare both sets of data. **[4 marks]**

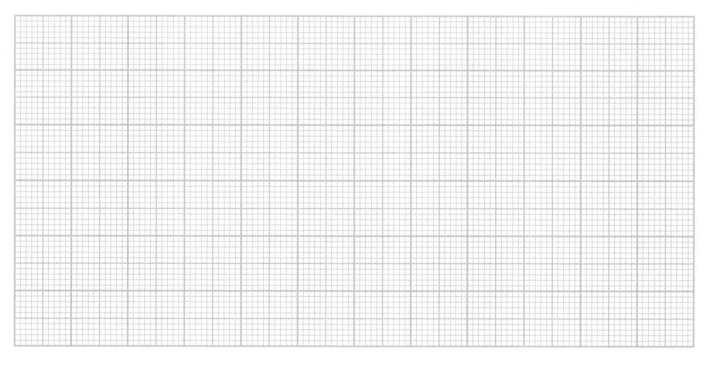

TURN OVER FOR THE NEXT PART OF THE QUESTION

(b) Comment on the difference between the lengths of telephone calls received by the two operatives.

[2 marks]

16 T is inversely proportional to R.

$T = 7$ when $R = 4$

(a) Work out the value of T when $R = 5$.

Answer _____ [2 marks]

(b) Work out the value of R when $T = 56$.

Answer _____ [2 marks]

(c) Sketch the graph of T against R on the axes below.

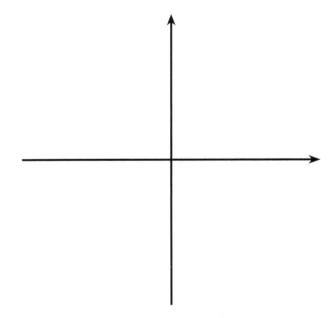

[2 marks]

17 The packaging for a chocolate bar is constructed using the net shown below.

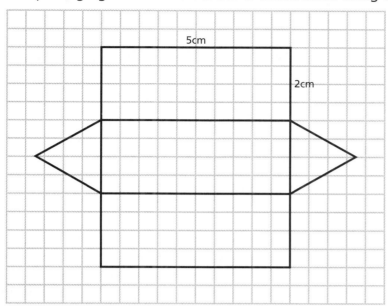

(a) Write down the name of the solid that can be made from this net.

Answer _____ **[1 mark]**

(b) The net shown is a scale drawing of the real net.

The ratio of the drawing to the real net is 1 : 3

(i) Calculate the height of the real solid once it is constructed.

Leave your answer in surd form.

Answer _____ **[3 marks]**

(ii) What is the ratio of the volume of the scale solid to the volume of the real solid?

Circle your answer.

1 : 9   1 : 3   1 : 6   1 : 27   **[1 mark]**

TURN OVER FOR THE NEXT PART OF THE QUESTION

(iii) Find the volume of the real solid once it is constructed.

Answer _____ **[2 marks]**

(iv) The packaging is cut from a rectangular strip of cardboard of lengths 26cm by 18cm.

Calculate the percentage of wastage of cardboard in this process.

Answer _____ **[4 marks]**

18 Solve $\dfrac{3}{x-1} + \dfrac{2}{2x+3} = 5$

Answer _____ **[4 marks]**

19 r and s are positive integers.

$11r + s$ is a multiple of 8.

Prove that $3r + s$ is also a multiple of 8.

Answer _____ **[2 marks]**

20 Five bags of sand and four bags of gravel weigh 340kg.

Three bags of sand and five bags of gravel weigh 321kg.

Ben buys six bags of sand and eight bags of gravel.

His van has a safe carrying load of 500kg.

Ben's friend, Sam, thinks it is not safe to travel.

Is Sam correct? Explain your answer.

[4 marks]

21 Simplify $\left(27x^3z^6\right)^{-\frac{1}{3}}$

Answer _____ [3 marks]

22 Convert the recurring decimal $0.\dot{5}\dot{7}$ to a fraction in its lowest terms.

Answer _____ [3 marks]

23 £5000 is invested at a compound interest rate of 4% per annum.

Work out the value of the investment after three years.

Answer _____ [2 marks]

TURN OVER FOR THE NEXT QUESTION

24   The following formula is used to calculate the density of an object:

Density $= \dfrac{\text{Mass}}{\text{Volume}}$

Mass = 540g to 2 significant figures.

Volume = 211.1cm³ to 1 decimal place.

Calculate the upper and lower bound of the density of the object.

Give your answers correct to 3 significant figures.

Upper Bound: _____ g/cm³

Lower Bound: _____ g/cm³   **[4 marks]**

END OF QUESTIONS

Answers

Workbook Answers

You are encouraged to show all your working out, as you may be awarded marks for method even if your final answer is wrong. Full marks can be awarded where a correct answer is given without working but, if a question asks for working, you must show it to gain full marks. If you use a correct method that is not shown in the answers below, you would still gain full credit for it.

Page 4 – Order and Value

1. a) 2×10^8 [1]
   b) 0.000678 [1]
2. $1.5 \times 10^4 = 15\,000$ [1]; $3.5 \times 10^3 = 3500$ [1]; 1.85×10^4 [1]
3. $\sqrt{m} = \sqrt{8100} = 90$ [1]; $\dfrac{3\sqrt{m}}{y} = \dfrac{270}{0.027}$ [1]; 1×10^4 [1]
4. a) 36.9 [1]
   b) 0.0369 [1]
5. 1.729 [2]
6. ▲ = 3 [1]

Page 5 – Types of Number

1. a) 3, 7, 31 [1]
   b) 3, 7 [1]
   c) 12, 16, 20 [1]
   d) 9, 16 [1]
   e) 20 [1]
2. $2 \times 2 \times 19$ OR $2^2 \times 19$ [2]
3. $684 = 2^2 \times 3^2 \times 19$ [1]; $468 = 2^2 \times 3^2 \times 13$ [1]; HCF $= 2^2 \times 3^2 = 36$ [1]
4. Sum of even numbers from 2 to 1000 = 250\,500, sum of odd numbers from 1 to 999 = 250\,000 [1]; 500 [1]

   Each even number minus the odd number immediately before it equals 1. Since there are 500 even numbers from 2 to 1000, $500 \times 1 = 500$.

5. No [1]; because 279 and 27 are not prime numbers [1]

Page 6 – Basic Algebra

1. $2x + 4 = 8$ [1]; $2x = 4$ [1]; $x = 2$ [1]
2. −60 [1]
3. $3x^2 - 3xy + xy + 5y$ [1]; $3x^2 - 2xy + 5y$ [1]
4. $2x = 12$ [1]; $x = 6$ [1]
5. $\dfrac{2}{x} = 18$ [1]; $x = \dfrac{1}{9}$ OR 0.111 [1]
6. $a = 3$, $b = 3$, $c = -1$, $d = 2$, $3y(3x - 1y + 2x^2)$ [2] (1 mark for 2–3 correct terms)

Page 7 – Factorisation and Formulae

1. $x^2 + 4x - 2x - 8$ [1]; $x^2 + 2x - 8$ [1]
2. $(2x + 1)(x + 2)$ [2] (1 mark for each correct bracket)
3. a) 40 [1]
   b) $v - u = at$ [1]; $t = \dfrac{v - u}{a}$ [1]
   c) 8.75 [1]
4. $pr + 2p = 3r - 1$ [1];
   THEN $2p + 1 = r(3 - p)$ [1]; $r = \dfrac{2p + 1}{3 - p}$ [1]

   OR $r(p - 3) = -1 - 2p$ [1]; $r = \dfrac{-1 - 2p}{p - 3}$ [1]

Page 8 – Ratio and Proportion

1. 5 : 2 [1]
2. $161.7 \div 11 = 14.7\text{km}$ [1]; $14.7 \times 13 = 191.1\text{km}$ [1]
3. 6 : 3 : 1, one share = £70 [1]; Sarah receives $6 \times £70 = £420$ [1]
4. 1 : 200 [1]
5. a) d is proportional to t^2 so $d = kt^2$ [1]; $k = 5$ [1]
   b) $48 = kt^2$; $48 = 5t^2$ [1]; $t = \sqrt{9.6} = 3.1$ seconds [1]

Page 9 – Variation and Compound Measures

1. $4000 \times (1 + \dfrac{1.6}{100})^3$ [1]; £4195.09 [1]; £4195 [1]
2. a) Speed $= 77.8 \div 8$ [1]; $= 9.725\text{m/s}$ [1]
   b) Speed $= 35010\text{m/h}$ [1]; Speed $= 35.01\text{km/h}$ [1]

   Speed = Distance ÷ Time

3. Volume $= 2 \div 10.49$ [1]; $= 0.191\text{cm}^3$ (to 3 decimal places) OR 0.19cm^3 (to 2 decimal places) [1]

   Volume = Mass ÷ Density

4. $F = \dfrac{k}{d^2} \rightarrow k = Fd^2$ [1]; $k = 12 \times 3^2$ [1]; $k = 108$ [1]

Page 10 – Angles and Shapes 1 & 2

1. $9x = 360°$ **[1]**; $x = 40°$ **[1]**
2. Exterior angle (= 180° − 150°) = 30° **[1]**;
   Number of sides = 360 ÷ 30 = 12 **[1]**
3. a) Correct scale drawing (see sketch below) **[1]**;
   Distance = 62km (+/− 2km) **[1]**

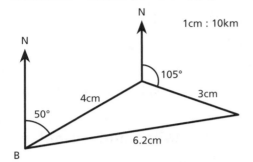

   b) Bearing 253° (+/− 2°) **[1]**

Page 11 – Fractions

1. $\dfrac{45}{63}$ **[1]**
2. $\dfrac{1}{3}$ left for the afternoon **[1]**; $\dfrac{2}{15}$ left for tomorrow **[1]**
3. $\dfrac{7}{9}$ of 81 = 63 **[1]**; $\dfrac{2}{7}$ of 217 = 62, so $\dfrac{7}{9}$ of 81 is larger **[1]**
4. 2.4 hours = 144 minutes **[1]**; $\dfrac{14}{144} = \dfrac{7}{72}$ **[1]**
5. $d = 0.272\,727\ldots$, $100d = 27.2727\ldots$ **[1]**;
   $99d = 27$ **[1]**; $d = \dfrac{27}{99} = \dfrac{3}{11}$ **[1]**
6. $\left(\dfrac{3}{2}\right)^{p} = \dfrac{3}{4} + \dfrac{3}{2} = \dfrac{9}{4}$ **[1]**; $p = 2$ **[1]**

Page 12 – Percentages

1. 20% increase = 180 **[1]**; 35% increase on 180 = 243 rats **[1]**
2. Convert 0.075kg to 75g **[1]**; $\dfrac{18}{75} \times 100 = 24\%$ **[1]**
3. $\dfrac{22}{100} \times c = 11$ **[1]**; $c = 50$ children **[1]**
4. $31 \times \dfrac{100}{62}$ OR 31 ÷ 0.62 **[1]**; 50 plants **[1]**
5. £280 **[1]**

Page 13 – Probability 1 & 2

1. a) $5x + 0.5 = 1$ **[1]**; $5x = 0.5$ **[1]**; $x = 0.1$ **[1]**
   b) No **[1]**; not all outcomes are equally likely **[1]**
2. a) $n - 8$ **[1]**; $\dfrac{n - 8}{n}$ **[1]**
   b) $\dfrac{5}{n} \times \dfrac{3}{n - 1} + \dfrac{3}{n} \times \dfrac{5}{n - 1}$ **[1]**; $= \dfrac{30}{n(n - 1)}$ **[1]**
3. a) 60, 15, 5 correct on diagram (see below).

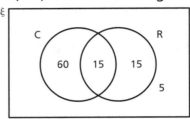

[1]

   b) $\dfrac{5}{95}$ **[1]**; $= \dfrac{1}{19}$ or 0.053 **[1]**
4. a) 0.82 **[1]**; Completely correct tree **[1]**

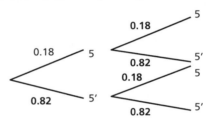

   b) $0.18 \times 0.82 = 0.1476$ **[1]**; 0.1476×2 **[1]**;
   = 0.2952 **[1]**

Page 15 – Number Patterns and Sequences & Terms and Rules

1. a) −1, −4 **[2]**
   b) $11 - 3n$ **[1]**
   c) No **[1]**; because n is not an integer when $11 - 3n = -15$ **[1]**
2. a) 48, 96 **[1]**
   b) $U_{n+1} = 2U_n$ **[1]**
3. 251 (nth term is $2n^3 + 1$) **[1]**
4. 5, 11, 29, 83, 245 **[2]** (1 mark for any three correct)

Page 16 – Transformations

1. a) Reflection **[1]**; in line $x = -\dfrac{1}{2}$ **[1]**
   b) Rotation **[1]**; anticlockwise 90° **[1]**; centre of rotation (0, 0) **[1]**
   c) Reflection **[1]**; in line $y = x$ **[1]**

2. One mark for each correct vertex of triangle *DEF* (all construction lines must be seen). **[3]**

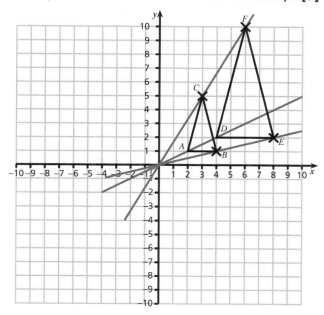

Page 17 – Constructions

1. Correct construction of the perpendicular bisector of *CD*. **[2]**

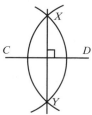

2. Correct construction of the bisectors of the three angles. **[3]**

3. Accurate rectangle 3cm by 4cm **[1]**; Diagonals of rectangle drawn. **[1]**

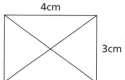

Page 18 – Linear Graphs

1. $m = -\dfrac{12}{4} = -3$ **[1]**; $c = 4$ **[1]**; $y = -3x + 4$ **[1]**

2. $-\dfrac{2}{5}$ **[1]**

3. $m = \dfrac{15 - 5}{6 - 1} = 2$ **[1]**; $5 = 2 \times 1 + c \rightarrow c = 3$ **[1]**;

   $y = 2x + 3$ **[1]**

4. $x + y = 5$ **[1]**; $x + y - 5 = 0$ **[1]**

Page 19 – Graphs of Quadratic Functions

1. a)

x	–2	–1	0	1	2
y	1	–5	–7	–5	1

[1]

   b) Points plotted accurately **[1]**; joined with a smooth curve. **[1]**

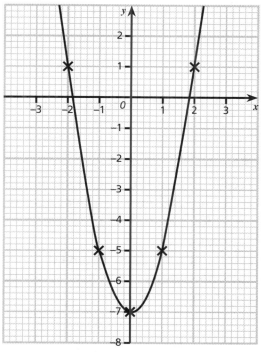

2. a) Maximum: (–2.5, 0.5) **[1]**;
      Minimum: (–1.25, –1.5) **[1]**

   b) Maximum: (0.75, 1.5) **[1]**;
      Minimum: (–0.5, –0.5) **[1]**

Page 20 – Powers, Roots and Indices

1. 4 **[1]**

2. $8x^6y^3$ (1 mark for each correct term) **[2]**

3. $\dfrac{3}{8}$ **[1]**

4. $\dfrac{\sqrt{3} - 1}{\sqrt{3}} \times \dfrac{\sqrt{3}}{\sqrt{3}}$ **[1]**; $\dfrac{3 - \sqrt{3}}{3}$ **[1]**

5. $\sqrt{3}\left(\sqrt{3} - 2\right)$ **[1]**; $3 - 2\sqrt{3}$ **[1]**

Page 21 – Area and Volume 1 & 2

1. Area of cross-section $= \dfrac{1}{2}(2.1 + 0.9) \times 25 = 37.5$,

   Volume $= 37.5 \times 10 = 375$ **[1]**;

   $375 \div 0.2 = 1875$ seconds **[1]**; $1875 \div 3600$ **[1]**

   $= 0.521$ hours (to 3 significant figures) **[1]**

   3600 seconds = 1 hour

2. $h = 3r$ **[1]**; $\pi r^2 (3r) = 275\pi$ **[1]**;

   $r = \sqrt[3]{\dfrac{275}{3}}$ **[1]**; $r = 4.51$ cm **[1]**

Page 22 – Uses of Graphs

1.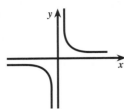
[1]

2. $m = -\frac{2}{3}$ [1]; $6 = -\frac{2}{3} \times 3 + c$ [1]; $c = 8$ [1];

$y = -\frac{2}{3}x + 8$ [1]

3. $M = 3$ [1]; The cost increases by 3p per minute. [1]

Page 23 – Other Graphs 1

1. a) Accelerates for the first 10 seconds, from stationary to 20m/s [1]; drives at a constant speed for 20 seconds [1]; decelerates for the next 40 seconds to 0m/s [1]
   b) $100 + 400 + 400$ [2]; $= 900m$ [1]

2. Correct y-intercept $(0, -1)$ [1]; correct shape of curve. [1]

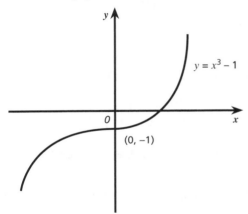

Page 24 – Other Graphs 2

1. $r = 3\sqrt{5}$ [1]

2. a) 9m/s [1]
   b) It reaches its highest point and is just about to begin dropping back down [1]
   c) $0.5 \times 3 \times 9$ [1]; $= 13.5m$ [1]

3. Gradient of radius $= \frac{7}{3}$ [1]; $m = -\frac{3}{7}$ [1];

$7 = -\frac{3}{7} \times 3 + c \rightarrow c = \frac{58}{7}$ [1]; $y = -\frac{3}{7}x + \frac{58}{7}$

OR $7y + 3x - 58 = 0$ [1]

Page 25 – Inequalities

1. a) $30 \ (-6 \times -5)$ [1]
   b) $-30 \ (-6 \times 5)$ [1]

2. $y > -6$ [1]; $y \leqslant 5$ [1]; $-5, -4, -3, -2, -1, 0, 1, 2, 3, 4, 5$ [1]

3. 1 mark for each correct line drawn: $x = 0$, $x + y = 10$, $y = x$ [3]; 1 mark for correctly shaded region. [1]

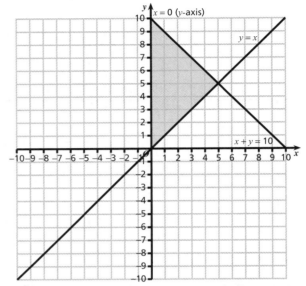

Page 26 – Congruence and Geometric Problems

1. a) A and B [1]; AAS or SAS [1]
   b) B and D [1]

2. $\frac{38}{2.8} = \frac{\text{lamp post height}}{1.6}$ or $(38 \div 2.8) \times 1.6$ [1]; $= 21.7$ metres [1]

3. Ratio of heights $= \frac{10}{8} = 1.25$ [1];
   Ratio of volumes $= 1.25 \times 1.25 \times 1.25$ [1];
   Volume of mug B $= 36 \div 1.25^3 = 18.432 = 18cm^3$ [1];
   OR
   Ratio of heights $= 1 : 0.8$ [1];
   Ratio of volumes $= 1 : 0.8^3$ [1];
   Volume of mug B $= 36 \times 0.8^3 = 18.432 = 18cm^3$ [1]

Page 27 – Right-Angled Triangles

1. $a^2 + a^2 = 16^2$ [1]; $2a^2 = 256$ [1]; $a = 11.31cm$ [1]

2. Longest diagonal of cuboid$^2 = 13^2 + 12^2 + 5^2$ [1];
   Longest diagonal of cuboid $= 18.38cm$ [1];
   Yes, 18cm pencil is shorter than the longest diagonal. [1]

3. $90° - 29° = 61°$, triangle ABC, $\tan 61° = \frac{AC}{20}$, AC is 36.0810m [1];

   Triangle ABD, $\tan 80° = \frac{AD}{20}$, $AD = 113.4256m$ [1]; $CD = 77m$ [1]

Page 28 – Sine and Cosine Rules

1. a) Use Cosine Rule: $a^2 = b^2 + c^2 - 2bc \cos A$ **[1]**;
   $a^2 = 32^2 + 19^2 - (2 \times 32 \times 19 \times \cos 47°)$ **[1]**;
   Distance apart = 23.57m **[1]**

   b) Area $= \frac{1}{2} bc \sin A = \frac{1}{2} \times 32 \times 19 \times \sin 47°$ **[1]**;
   $= 222m^2$ **[1]**

   c) 23.57m = 2357cm **[1]**;
   Time taken $2357 \div 40 = 58.925$ seconds **[1]**

2. Use Sine Rule: $\dfrac{EF}{\sin 52°} = \dfrac{32}{\sin 67°}$ **[1]**;
   $EF = 27.4$m **[1]**; Rope needed $=$
   $32 + 30.4 + 27.4 = 89.8$m **[1]**

Page 29 – Statistics 1

1. a) Point plotted at (15, 46) **[1]**
   b) Positive **[1]**
   c) Increase in time studying leads to increase in mark. **[1]**
   d) Line drawn (see diagram below) **[1]**
   e) 28–32 minutes **[1]**

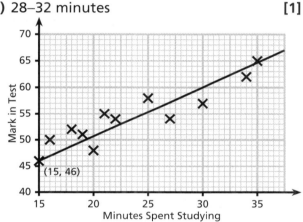

2. $15.2 \times 23 = 349.6$ **[1]**; $349.6 - 21.3 + 12.3$
   $= 340.6$ **[1]**; $340.6 \div 23 = 14.8$ **[1]**

Page 30 – Statistics 2

1. a) 14.3 – 14.7mm **[1]**
   b) 2.3 – 2.7mm **[1]**
   c) Correctly drawn lower quartile line and upper quartile line at either end of box **[2]**; correctly drawn median line **[1]**

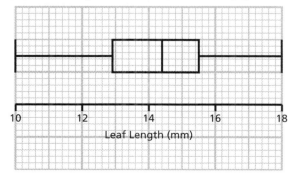

Leaf Length (mm)

d) Tree 2 on average has longer leaves (higher median) **[1]**; Tree 2 has a greater interquartile range – more variety of lengths. **[1]**

Page 31 – Measures, Accuracy and Finance

1. $(10 \times 1) \div (0.5)$ **[1]**; $= 20$ **[1]**; OR $(9 \times 1) \div (0.5)$ **[1]**;
   $= 18$ **[1]**

2. a) £23 + £12.50 + £8.70 **[1]**; = £44.20 **[1]**

   > Read the question carefully. The prices given were for a two-way trip and the question asks for costs for a single trip.

   b) $(3 \times 12.5) + 60 + 30 = 127.5$ euros **[1]**;
   127.5 euros = £99.45 **[1]**

3. Largest area $= 6.5 \times 7.5 = 48.75cm^2$ **[1]**;
   Smallest area $= 5.5 \times 6.5 = 35.75cm^2$ **[1]**

Page 32 – Solving Quadratic Equations

1. a) $(x + 1)^2 - 1 - 5 = 0$, $(x + 1)^2 - 6 = 0$ **[1]**;
   $p = 1$, $q = -6$ **[1]**
   b) $(x + 1)^2 = 6$ **[1]**; $x = -1 \pm \sqrt{6}$ **[1]**
   c) $(-1, -6)$ **[1]**

2. a) $P = 4(x + 3)$ **[1]**; $A = (x + 3)(x + 3)$ **[1]**;
   $4x + 12 = x^2 + 6x + 9$ **[1]**;
   $x^2 + 2x - 3 = 0$ **[1]**
   b) $(x + 3)(x - 1) = 0$ **[1]**; $x = 1$,
   length = 4cm **[1]**

Page 33 – Simultaneous Equations and Functions

1. $x^2 + (x + 2)^2 = 10$ **[1]**; $2x^2 + 4x - 6 = 0$ OR
   $x^2 + 2x - 3 = 0$ **[1]**;
   $(x + 3)(x - 1)$, $x = -3$ or $x = 1$ **[1]**;
   $y = -1$ or $y = 3$ **[1]**

2. a) 14 **[1]**
   b) $(3x + 5)^2 - 2(3x + 5)$ **[1]**; $9x^2 + 24x + 15$ **[1]**
   c) $(3x + 5)(x + 1) = 0$ **[1]**; $x = -\dfrac{5}{3}$, $x = -1$ **[1]**

Page 34 – Algebraic Proof

1. $(2a - 1)^2 - (2b - 1)^2 = 4a^2 - 4a + 1 -$
   $(4b^2 - 4b + 1)$ **[1]**; $= 4a^2 - 4a - 4b^2 + 4b$ **[1]**;
   $= 4(a^2 - a - b^2 + b)$ **[1]**;
   $= 4(a - b)(a + b + 1)$ **[1]**

2. $(2n + 3)^2 - (2n + 1)^2$ **[1]**; $= 4n^2 + 12n +$ $9 - (4n^2 + 4n + 1)$ **[1]**; $= 8n + 8$ **[1]**; $= 8(n + 1)$, a multiple of 8 **[1]**

3. Let $x = 0.888\ 888\ 88\ldots$ **[1]**; $10x = 8.888\ 888\ 888\ldots$ **[1]**; $9x = 8$ **[1]**, $x = \dfrac{8}{9}$ **[1]**

Page 35 – Circles

1. Angle $DEA = 90°$, so angle $DAE = 36°$ **[1]**; Angle $BAD = 70°$ (opposite angles of a cyclic quadrilateral add up to 180°) **[1]**; Angle BAE $= 70° + 36° = 106°$ **[1]**

2. $\dfrac{1}{2}(6d - 30°) = d + 17°$, so $3d - 15° = d + 17°$ OR equivalent **[1]**; $d = 16°$ **[1]**

3. $a = 16°$ **[1]**; $b = 16°$ **[1]**; $c = 74°$ **[1]**

Page 36 – Vectors

1. $\overrightarrow{KL}$, $\overrightarrow{MN}$, $\overrightarrow{ST}$ **[2]**; $\overrightarrow{OP}$, $\overrightarrow{QR}$ **[1]**

2. a) $4\mathbf{m}$ **[1]**
   b) $-2\mathbf{n}$ **[1]**
   c) $3\mathbf{m} - \mathbf{n}$ **[1]**
   d) $\mathbf{n} + \mathbf{m}$ **[1]**

3. Trapezium   **[1]**

Page 37 – Exam Practice Paper 1 (Non-Calculator)

1. $P = \dfrac{F}{A}$ **[1]**

2. $\dfrac{1}{2}$ **[1]**

3. $x^3 + 6x^2 + 11x + 6$ **[1]**

4. n^2 **[1]**

5. (a) $999\ 999$ **[1]**
   (b) (i) 27 **[1]** (ii) 25 **[1]** (iii) 60 **[1]**
   (c) True: 1 mark for any two correct answers, e.g. 5 and 7 **[1]**; Not true: 1 mark for any two correct answers, e.g. 11 and 23 **[1]**

6. 1.537 **[2]** (only award 1 mark if decimal point is in incorrect place)

7. (a) $a^2b = \dfrac{1}{16}$ **[1]**; $\dfrac{3}{16}$ **[1]**
   (b) $m = 3$ **[1]**
   (c) $p = 2$ **[1]**

8. Exterior angle of hexagon $= 360 \div 6 = 60°$ **[1]**; Interior angle $= 180 - 60 = 120°$ **[1]**; $\dfrac{1}{2}y = 180 - 120 = 60°$ **[1]**; $y = 120°$ **[1]**

9. (a) Correct drawing of triangle A (see diagram).   **[2]**
   (b) Correct reflection in y-axis to produce triangle B (see diagram).   **[2]**

(c) Correct rotation of triangle B to produce triangle C (see diagram).   **[2]**

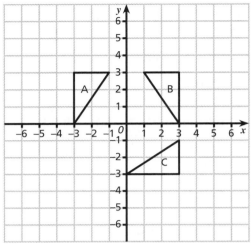

(d) Reflection in $y = x$ **[2]**

10. £1064 in the ratio of 8 : 6 **[1]**; 1 part $=$ £1064 $\div$ 14 $=$ £76 **[1]**; One man receives £76 $\times$ 8 $=$ £608 **[1]**; The other receives £76 $\times$ 6 $=$ £456 **[1]**

> This could also have been solved using the ratio 4 : 3, where 1 part $=$ £152

11. (a) True   **[1]**
   (b) False   **[1]**
   (c) True   **[2]**
   (d) True   **[2]**

12. (a) $(50 \times 100) \div (80 + 20)$ **[1]** $= 50$ (or estimate reasonably near to this) **[1]**
   (b) $x = 32\,000$, $y = 230\,000$ **[1]**; $x + y = 2.62 \times 10^5$ **[1]**
   (c) $0.000\ 681$ **[1]**
   (d) 10   **[1]**

13. (a) Correct y-intercept $(0, 1)$ **[1]**; all other points accurately plotted. **[1]**

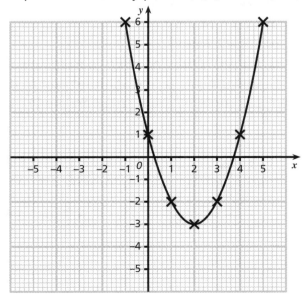

(b) $x = 3.7$ (+/− 0.2) **[1]**; $x = 0.3$ (+/− 0.2) **[1]**

(c) $x = 2$ **[2]**

14. (a) $3y^2$ **[1]**

(b) $4 - 2m^2 - 6m$ **[2]**

(c) $p^2 - pt + tp - t^2$ **[1]**; $(p + t)(p - t)$ **[1]**

(d) $3a^2 + 2a - 12a - 8$ **[1]**; $3a^2 - 10a - 8$ **[1]**

15. (a) $\frac{2}{8} \times \frac{1}{7}$ **[2]**; $\frac{2}{56} = \frac{1}{28}$ **[1]**

(b) $\frac{2}{8} \times \frac{6}{7} + \frac{6}{8} \times \frac{2}{7}$ **[1]**; $\frac{12}{56} + \frac{12}{56}$ **[1]**;

$\frac{24}{56} = \frac{3}{7}$ **[1]**

16. (a) 1 **[1]**

(b) 8 **[1]**

(c) $\frac{1}{7}$ **[1]**

(d) 8 **[1]**

(e) 10^3 **[1]**; = 1000 **[1]**

17. (a) 6, 10, 19, 29, 42, 60, 74, 88, 95, 100 **[2]**

(b) Correct scale and labels on axes **[1]**; Correct plotting of cumulative frequency curve. **[1]**

(c) Median = 55cm (+/− 5cm) **[1]**

(d) Interquartile range = 34cm (+/− 6cm) **[2]**

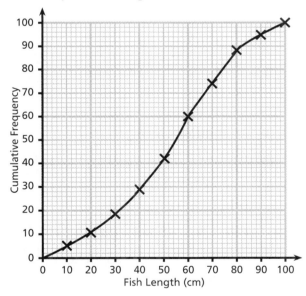

18. $\dfrac{1}{a + 2} + \dfrac{a}{(a + 2)(a + 4)}$ **[1]**;

$= \dfrac{(a + 4) + a}{(a + 2)(a + 4)}$ **[1]**; $= \dfrac{2a + 4}{(a + 2)(a + 4)}$ **[1]**;

$= \dfrac{2}{a + 4}$ **[1]**

Page 51 – Exam Practice Paper 2 (Calculator)

1. 2.1×10^8 **[1]**

2. 4 **[1]**

3. $p(c - d)$ **[1]**

4. 5400 **[1]**

5. (a) 61.0687 **[1]**

(b) 61.07 **[1]**

6. (a) $D = \frac{M}{V}$, $V = 270\,000 \div 7.5$ **[1]**; $36\,000\text{cm}^3$ **[1]**

(b) Length = $36\,000 \div 12 = 3000$cm **[1]** = 30m **[1]**

7. (a) $40^2 + 15^2 = x^2$ **[1]**; $x = 42.72$km **[2]**

(b) $\tan\theta = \frac{40°}{15}$ **[1]**; $\theta = 69°$ **[1]**;
Bearing = 090° + 069° = 159° **[1]**

8. Correct construction of equilateral triangle. **[2]**

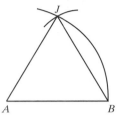

9. $5x - 2y = 8$ (× 3) = $15x - 6y = 24$, $7x + 3y = 17$ (× 2) = $14x + 6y = 34$, $29x = 58$, $x = 2$ **[2]**;
$7x + 3y = 17$, $14 + 3y = 17$, $y = 1$ **[2]**

10. (a) $1400 \times 2400 \times 140$ **[1]** = 470 400 litres **[1]**

(b) 235 200 seconds **[1]**; 3920 minutes = 65 hours **[2]**

(c) $14.2 \times 24.2 \times 1.5 = 515.46\text{m}^3$ **[1]**;
$14 \times 24 \times 1.4 = 470.4\text{m}^3$ **[1]**; 45.06m^3 **[1]**

11. 1 mile in 239 seconds **[1]**; 15.063mph **[1]**; 24.1km/h **[2]**

12. (a) $2 = 3m$ **[1]**; $m = \frac{2}{3}$ OR 0.67 **[1]**

(b) $q = 2(p - 1)$ OR $q = 2p - 2$ **[2]**

13. (a) $2(3 + x) + 2(4 + x)$ **[1]**; $4x + 14$ **[1]**

(b) $4x + 14 = 24$, $x = 2.5$m **[1]**;
Area = $22 + 7.5 = 29.5\text{m}^2$ **[1]**

(c) 12% of £24 = £2.88 **[1]**; $29.5 \times £21.12 = £623.04$ **[1]**; Yes, £625 > £623.04 **[1]**

14. (a) $\frac{21}{24} \times 100\%$ **[1]** = 87.5% **[1]**

(b) Area of ends = $\pi \times r \times r \times 2 = 157.1\text{cm}^2$ **[2]**; Total surface area = $157.1 + (3.142 \times 10 \times 10) = 471.3\text{cm}^2$ **[2]**

(c) $471.3 \times 60 = 28\,278\text{cm}^2 = 2.8278\text{m}^2$ **[2]**; Cost = $20 \times 2.8278 = 57$p **[2]**

15. (a) 54° **[1]**

(b) 90° **[1]**

(c) 90° **[1]**

(d) 126° **[1]**

16. $3000 \times (1.02)^6 = £3378.487$ **[2]**; £378.49 **[2]**

17. $a = 1$, $b = -5$ and $c = 3$ **[1]**;

$x = \dfrac{5 \pm \sqrt{(-5)^2 - 4 \times 1 \times 3}}{2 \times 1}$ **[1]**;

$x = 0.697$ **[1]**; $x = 4.30$ **[1]**

18. Cosine rule $GA^2 = 4.8^2 + 1.6^2 - 2 \times 4.8 \times 1.6 \times \cos 40°$ (Angle $GHA = 40°$) **[2]**; Distance $GA = 3.719$km **[2]**

19. $h = kt^2$ **[1]**; $k = 0.5$ **[1]**; $h = 128$m **[1]**

20. Gradient $= -\frac{1}{4}$ **[1]**; $y = -\frac{1}{4}x + 4$ **[2]**

21. **(a)** Perimeter $= 2(12+\sqrt{7})+2(12-\sqrt{7})$
    $= 48$ units **[1]**
    (b) Area $= (12+\sqrt{7})(12-\sqrt{7})$ **[1]**;
    Area $= 137$ square units **[1]**

Page 65 – Exam Practice Paper 3 (Calculator)

1. $-5 < x \leqslant 4$ **[1]**
2. $\frac{17}{3}$ **[1]**
3. 7 **[1]**
4. 2 and 3 **[1]**
5. $3x + 6 = 4x - 20$ **[1]**; $x = 26$ **[1]**
6. $4y(y - 4)$ **[2]** OR $4(y^2 - 4y)$ **[1]**
   OR $y(4y - 4)$ **[1]**
7. $6g + g + 8 = 4(g + 8) + (g + 8)$ **[1]**; $7g + 8 = 5g + 40$, $2g = 32$, $g = 16$ **[1]**; therefore, $b = 6 \times 16 = 96$, there are 96 boys. **[1]**

   Let g represent the number of girls. The ratio is 6 : 1, so the number of boys is $6g$.

8. $3x + 2 = 7x - 8$ **[1]**; $4x = 10$ **[1]**; $x = 2.5$ **[1]**
9. $\frac{20}{18} = \frac{17 + x}{17}$ **[1]**; $17 + x = \frac{170}{9}$ **[1]**; $x = \frac{17}{9}$ cm
   OR 1.89cm **[1]**
10. $(\sqrt{5})^2 + (\sqrt{10})^2 = y^2$ **[1]**; $5 + 10 = y^2$ **[1]**;
    $y = \sqrt{15}$ OR 3.87 **[1]**
11. **(a)** $\frac{3}{20} \times \frac{2}{19} \times \frac{1}{18}$ **[1]** $= \frac{1}{1140}$ **[1]**
    (b) $\frac{3}{20} \times \frac{17}{19} \times \frac{16}{18}$ **[1]**; $\frac{3}{20} \times \frac{17}{19} \times \frac{16}{18} \times 3$ **[1]**;
    $\frac{34}{95}$ **[1]**
12. **(a)** $\frac{27}{100}$ OR 0.27 **[1]**
    (b) $\frac{31}{100} \times 600$ **[1]**; $= 186$ **[1]**
13. $AC = 3\mathbf{b} - 3\mathbf{a}$ **[1]**; $AB = \mathbf{b} - \mathbf{a}$ **[1]**;
    $AC = 3AB$, therefore straight line **[1]**
14. $AC = \sqrt{72}$ **[1]**; $h^2 = 36 - 18$, $h = \sqrt{18}$ **[1]**;
    $V = \frac{1}{3} \times 36 \times \sqrt{18}$ **[1]**; $V = 50.9$cm³
    (to 3 significant figures) **[1]**

15. **(a)** Correctly plotted lower and upper quartiles for Ben **[1]**; correctly plotted median line for Ben **[1]**; Correctly plotted lower and upper quartiles for Bill **[1]**; correctly plotted median line for Bill. **[1]**

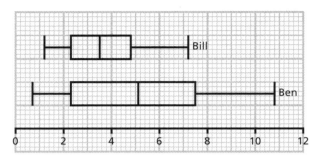

(b) On average Ben has longer phone calls **[1]**; The length of Bill's phone calls is more consistent. **[1]**

16. **(a)** $T = \frac{28}{R}$ **[1]**; $T = 5.6$ **[1]**
    (b) $56 = \frac{28}{R}$ **[1]**; $R = 0.5$ **[1]**
    (c) One mark for each correctly plotted curve. **[2]**

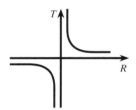

17. **(a)** Triangular prism **[1]**
    (b) **(i)** $\sqrt{2^2 - 1^2} = \sqrt{3}$ **[1]**; $\sqrt{3} \times 3$ **[1]**;
    $3\sqrt{3}$ cm **[1]**
    (ii) 1 : 27 **[1]**
    (iii) $V = \frac{1}{2} \times 5 \times 2 \times \sqrt{3} = 5\sqrt{3}$ cm³ **[1]**;
    $5\sqrt{3} \times 3^3 = 233.83.$cm³ **[1]**
    (iv) $26 \times 18 = 468$cm²
    (area of rectangle) **[1]**;
    $3 \times 15 \times 6 + 2 \times \frac{1}{2} \times 6 \times 3\sqrt{3} =$
    $270 + 31.1769 = 301.1769$ **[1]**;
    $\frac{301.7679}{468} \times 100 = 64.4\%$ **[1]**;
    $100 - 64.4 = 35.6\%$ wastage **[1]**

18. $3(2x + 3) + 2(x - 1) = 5(x - 1)(2x + 3)$ **[1]**; $10x^2 - 3x - 22 = 0$ **[1]**; solve by quadratic formula **[1]**; $x = 1.64$ and $x = -1.34$ **[1]**

19. $11r + s - (3r + s)$ **[1]** $= 8r$, which is a multiple of 8 **[1]**

20. $5s + 4g = 340$ and $3s + 5g = 321$ **[1]**; Solve to find $g = 45$ and $s = 32$ **[1]**; $6 \times 32 + 8 \times 45 = 552$ **[1]**; 552 greater than 500, so Sam is correct. **[1]**

21. $\frac{1}{3}x^{-1}z^{-2}$ **[3]** OR $\frac{1}{3xz^2}$ **[3]**

22. $x = 0.575757\ldots$ **[1]**; $100x = 57.5757\ldots$ so $99x = 57$ **[1]**; $x = \frac{19}{33}$ **[1]**

23. $5000 \times (1.04)^3$ **[1]**; $= £5624.32$ **[1]**

24. 535 and 545 **[1]**; 211.05 and 211.15 **[1]**; UB = 2.58g/cm³ (to 3 significant figures) **[1]**; LB = 2.53g/cm³ (to 3 significant figures) **[1]**

Notes

Notes

Acknowledgements

The author and publisher are grateful to the copyright holders for permission to use quoted materials and images.

All images are © Shutterstock.com

Every effort has been made to trace copyright holders and obtain their permission for the use of copyright material. The author and publisher will gladly receive information enabling them to rectify any error or omission in subsequent editions. All facts are correct at time of going to press.

Published by Collins

An imprint of HarperCollins*Publishers*

1 London Bridge Street
London SE1 9GF

© HarperCollins*Publishers* Limited 2015

ISBN 9780008326654

Content first published 2015
This edition published 2018

10 9 8 7 6 5 4 3 2 1

British Library Cataloguing in Publication Data.

A CIP record of this book is available from the British Library.

Commissioning Editors: Rebecca Skinner and Emily Linnett
Project Leader: Richard Toms
Project Management: Rebecca Skinner
Authors: Linda Couchman and Rebecca Evans
Cover Design: Sarah Duxbury and Paul Oates
Inside Concept Design: Sarah Duxbury and Paul Oates
Text Design and Layout: Jouve India Private Limited
Production: Lyndsey Rogers
Printed by Martins the Printers